TESTIMONIALS

"I have had the great pleasure in knowing Colleen for many years. As an award winning entrepreneur. I've learned that the key to success is to partner with EXPERTS. Colleen is one such expert.

In a community of thousands of options, having an expert to help you filter the "BEST" from the rest is extremely valuable. Colleen's expertise has garnered her both the respect of her clients as well as her colleagues. As such she has become a very valuable asset to anyone hoping to avoid VERY costly mistakes.

One will never be able to eliminate risk... but one can minimize that risk while also maximizing the potential for success by finding the 'RIGHT" business. Working with Colleen will be one of the best decisions you'll EVER make!!!!"

~Larry Carnell, Vice President, Benetrends;
Award Winning Entrepreneur

"I have known Colleen O'Brien for the past 8 years. It didn't take me too long to label her as the "consummate broker." She is not only extremely knowledgeable about the franchising business, but has an abundant amount of compassion for both the franchisor and also the franchisee. She is truly a treat to work with."

~Tom Lamb, COO of Kona Ice

"Colleen is a MASTER of franchising. She understands what it takes to be successful and is willing to share her years of experience with those willing to listen."

~Heidi Morrissey, VP Marketing/Sales , Kitchen Tune-Up

"In my experience in the franchising world, taking a concept to over 700 franchises, I have interacted with numerous franchise experts. The multiple conferences and franchising seminars I have attended are crowded with intelligent people that are savvy in this industry. I can honestly say that although there are many good people in the industry the true professionals are rare. Colleen O'Brien is that rare exception. Her insight and discernment navigating the ocean of candidates coming into and "looking" at franchises is quite remarkable. Her understanding of the entire process is what makes her rare."

~Tony Lamb, CEO and Founder of Kona Ice

THE FRANCHISE GAME

Discover the 7 Strategic Moves to Buying
A Winning Franchise

COLLEEN L. O'BRIEN

Published by the Barnum Media Group

BARNUM
Media Group

17701 108th Ave SE #133
Renton, WA 98055 USA
Phone: (425) 202-5854
Email: info@BarnumMedia.com
www.BarnumMedia.com

Composition and design: Barnum Media Group

Printed in the United States of America
First Printing, 2016
ISBN 978-0-9963911-8-4

Ordering Information

Special discounts are available on quantity purchases by corporations, associations, and other organizations. For details, contact the publisher at the address above.

About the Author

My name is Colleen L. O'Brien. If you found this book, then you have likely been looking for a business. Let me first say I am not exactly the best writer in the world, but please try to see the forest through the trees as you read this book. You will find it to be conversational and full of pertinent information necessary to successfully buy a franchise.

I have played franchise matchmaker for folks like you since 2004. Prior to that, my career was in Management Consulting and Project Management. For those interested in education credentials, I graduated in 1993 from the Kellogg Graduate School of Management at Northwestern University, and received my undergraduate degree in 1987 in Business and Industrial Management from Purdue University.

I did what we are all taught to do. I studied in school, went to college, and got a good job. For my career, an MBA was essential, so I did that. I went to school at night while working full time. Hard work, but it was an exhilarating time!

I had numerous rewarding experiences in my career, but I wanted more. In 2003, I managed the shut-down of my employer due to a merger. It was a horrible experience and I promised myself that I would not do that again. I took my severance and became self-employed – and I have not turned back!

I became a Franchise Coach given my business experience and education. A Franchise Coach is much like a recruiter in the corporate world, we just match you to a franchise instead of a job, and the services are free. How is it free? I am paid by the franchise company should we find a franchise for you to purchase. No additional funds are required to purchase the franchise as well. Franchise Coaches are also called Franchise Brokers, and some say Franchise Consultant. I use the term Franchise Coach since it is a better fit with the role played. It is much more than just giving a candidate a list of franchises to review.

I wanted to learn all that I could about the business world and being an entrepreneur. I realized over the years that being a Franchise Coach is a nice fit for me for now. I love solving problems, which is what I do every day – finding the right business for those struggling to find one.

I also progressed into Franchise Sales and Development. Basically, I help franchise companies award a franchise to the best qualified and interested candidates. What an eye-opening experience. It is a fast paced and highly-energized environment, but I also have realized so many qualified people go about the research process all wrong. Hence, I wrote this book to help those of you struggling to get into business – to find the right business!

I am also not a stranger to being a franchisee. My husband and I are franchisees with a large third-party logistics company – Unishippers. This company is a solid fit for us given we wanted a home based, business-to-business operation that primarily leveraged sales skills.

I have truly seen the Franchise Sales from all perspectives, and I am ready to help you.

So let's get started! Let me help you follow the rules and start the game right so you can pick a winner.

Table of Contents

Introduction

After reading this book, you should have a better understanding of whether you would make a solid business owner, and if so, what kind of business format you should pursue. Once that is decided, you will be better equipped to research the right type of business. You will be able to do it in such a way that you will make an informed decision and, more importantly, win the game of finding a business.

This book is focused on the franchise world, but don't let that stop you from completing it if you are looking into another form of business. Much of what you learn in this book can apply to various business formats, especially the review of online opportunities. The frustration seems to come when trying to find a franchise.

I have been in the franchise world since 2004 in various capacities and I have seen franchise prospects make every mistake possible while attempting to research franchises. They are especially frustrated when they think they found the right one, yet they cannot get the information they expect and they think they are doing the right things.

This book will help you to attack the process with new energy, and with the criteria and resources needed to streamline the search and help you to be awarded the franchise that is best for you. Note I said "awarded." If that term raises questions for you – then all the more reason to keep reading!

I hope you will see that the review process really is more of a game, and there are rules to be followed in the game. The problem, though, is that the rules are not spelled out. Many are surprised to learn that the rules mostly require common courtesy. If we can correct some of the misconceptions that most candidates have about the process, we can hopefully see a healthy expansion in the industry for those truly wanting a franchise business.

This is not a long book because I know you want to get to the steps and own a business. With the right focus and assistance, you will be prepared to make a purchase decision and become a business owner. So let's get to it!

USE THIS VALUABLE FREE WORKSHEET TO FIND YOUR WINNING FRANCHISE

Download This Free Worksheet Now!

www.TheFranchiseGame.com/bonus

Know *Why* You Want Your Own Business

*"I am not a product of my circumstances.
I am a product of my decisions."*

–Stephen Covey

Why do we have such a small percentage of individuals going into business for themselves? And of those who do, why do so many fail? I would contend that most people do not take enough time to understand their true "WHY," followed by "WHAT" they can truly handle doing on a day-to-day basis and what they can afford.

When most of us envision having our own business, we picture freedom. This could mean more money, more time, or both. That is often the top reason WHY one may want a business. But one should look much more deeply for the WHY so that person remains motivated when the going gets tough for WHAT he or she chooses to do.

The Dream

One of the first questions I ask business candidates is this: "Why do you want to have your own business?" A massive majority reply: "I have always dreamt of having my own business." This is a nice start, but we need to go deeper. You need to visualize what will truly be different. Everyone wants more money and more time, but those are not detailed enough to make a decision on a business. Here are lifestyle elements to consider:

- Golf regularly, including trips away from home
- Lounge at the pool with your kids over summer break
- Send your children to the college of their choice – with no loans
- Travel to exotic places on a whim
- Spoil your grandchildren with all that they desire
- Have the money and time to attend the emergency funeral that just entered your calendar this week
- Donate a large sum of money anonymously to a worthy charity
- Pick up your kids each day from school and help them with their homework

Doesn't it all sound wonderful? And it is all possible.

A common misconception is that having your own business **instantly** gives you these things. It can happen, but the more instantaneous you want it to be, the more expensive it will be. You could buy a business that generates a $500,000 income, but that will come at a price.

Being a business owner can be rewarding. The question is – are you serious? It is not something to take lightly if you are adamant about being financially self-sustaining. One major hurdle in the entire search is committing to the search, and being serious about being a business owner.

When I ask prospective business owners why they want their own businesses, 93 percent of them will say "I want more freedom." This is GREAT! However, we need more. Get to the true "why":

What will be different in your life? Consider this in both the short term and long term.

Are you willing to make sacrifices now, both in time and money, to gain that freedom down the road?

If you stopped working today, how long would your money last? What can you do to extend that time? (Get creative – refinance your mortgage, sell a vehicle, turn down the heat, eat hamburger instead of steak, etc.)

What are you missing out on today that is a top priority to stop missing? Maybe you are tired of traveling? Maybe you hate working nights? Are you in customer service but would rather be creative and make things?

These sound simple, but in reality, most of us who start the search for a business do not truly think about these things. We want "the next hot thing," not realizing that the hot thing could be a flash in the pan and gone tomorrow. These can be fun, but they are for the true entrepreneur, willing to take higher risks. These are the things to think about, and to learn more about what is important to you.

Determine What You Want

I have found that a great place to start is with your family, occupation, and recreation. You need to note what you want and don't want, or like and don't like, about these categories. Next, how do you want them to change if you have your own business?

Here are starting points for each category:

Family

What do you enjoy doing together?

What do you despise doing together?

What is missing – how do you want your time together to change?

If you are married, do you want to have your spouse in the business, or will you be oil and water working together?

If you have children, do you want them involved if they are old enough? Is it a goal to pass this business down to your children?

Occupation

What do you do for a living now? If you sell – don't just say sales. What do you sell? How do you make a difference?

Where do you excel in your profession?

Where could you improve?

What do you love about what you do? What is the most rewarding?

What do you despise about your job?

Recreation

What do you do for fun?

Can you make money doing what you love?

Have you ever had ideas related to what you enjoy that could be a business, but you never pursued it?

Hopefully this is getting your creative juices flowing about what you want and don't want in a business. Sometimes we know more about what we don't want, and it leads us to what we do want.

Example

Jenny manages the customer service department for a large insurance company. Since she is the manager, she works long hours from 7 A.M. to 6 P.M. every day. She misses out on numerous activities with her children, and now she bitterly arrives in her office every day. Her husband, Eric, has a nice career in IT, and he is content. It would be tight, but they can make it just on Eric's salary for about nine months. They have saved $75,000 over the years, and they feel they can devote $50,000 to a business for Jenny to operate.

Jenny enjoys being with people, but she is also tired of managing employees that do not care, or don't show up for work. She would like to avoid this scenario in a new business. Jenny enjoys decorating and wishes she had more time to do so in her own home.

Over the past year, she has scanned the internet for various food franchises that were familiar to her. She especially liked the frozen yogurt franchises. Each time she inquired, the sales person would tell her she was not qualified financially, as a frozen yogurt location typically requires at least $100,000 in liquid cash to qualify.

Believe it or not – there is a perfect franchise segment for Jenny in the window covering business. Tell me you ever would have thought that selling window treatments in the home would be a nice business for her, or that you personally would have even inquired about this business. It is a nice Monday through Friday business with custom solutions, so there is little to no inventory. She receives 50 percent down on the orders, so she is not out the money herself for her product. There are a few options in this segment, and we would need to check territory availability and match to a few other characteristics. Encouraging, isn't it?

The Perfect Business

Is the perfect business out there? It can be. We all have this vision of going to work, doing what we love.

Here is a reality: often what we LOVE will not make us money – at least not right away – and keep the lights on. At least three times a day when I am counseling clients on the right business, they will say, "I have to do something that I love" or "I have to be passionate about it." It boils down to the resources you have available to invest in a business, with your current skill set, if you can do what you love as business.

Have you taken time to reflect on what you wanted to do upon entering college, and how much that college education cost you? Are you still pursuing that career?

One of the best books to read regarding what it takes to have your own business is called *The E-Myth* by Michael E. Gerber. This book illustrates why so many people fail in business. He shows why a woman who loved baking pies struggled with her new pie store, and what she needed to do to overcome it. Though he does not say you need to buy a franchise, he gives a mountain of evidence why a franchise can be the way to go. A solid franchise has the recipe for success and what you need to do, step by step. And he shows how you can duplicate that system successfully and repeatedly. Isn't that what we are looking to do in a business? And isn't that what a franchise is all about? Using someone else's proven system?

I often recommend that individuals look at building multiple streams of income. This is helpful if a candidate has little money to spare and invest in a business. *Rich Dad Poor Dad* by Robert Kyosaki is another great read to understand the basics. He explains moving from an employee to a business owner. There are steps involved, and the ultimate goal is to build businesses that can run without you being there. This gets us to "The Dream" at the beginning of this section. It can take a while to get there, and many of us need to crawl before we walk. That may mean a smaller version of a business as a first step.

My message is this – the business world is often different from what the current non-business owner realizes. It is an exhilarating environment, and I believe that just about anyone willing to learn and to be coached can have a thriving business. It just may look differently than you originally pictured. Taking the time to understand more about yourself will keep you from breaking the bank later down the road.

Uncertainty and Fear

You would be amazed at the "reasons" a candidate will give when deciding against a business, or against going into business altogether. I am constantly amazed at the number of family illnesses that suddenly take the complete attention of a franchise candidate. This is especially true when we are at the end of the process and a go/no go decision is required. I know what you are thinking – how cold! Now, before you throw this book at the wall and call me insensitive, know this – I fully know that family situations arise and people get sick. However, the volume that occurs suddenly at decision time is astounding.

The candidate just does not want to verbalize the true issue. Either the person doesn't want to do the business or, more likely, the business really is a nice fit and he or she cannot pull the trigger. And why not? Because of uncertainty and fear.

Even if you talk with each franchisee in a franchise system, and each sings the praises of the franchisor, making that final decision to move forward can paralyze the first-time business owner.

Fear is something that you need to acknowledge, and let guide you. It means you have questions that still must be answered.

We are all concerned about failing. Most franchise systems will have locations close and shut down. I would encourage you **not** to assume that it was due to the franchise. Most of the time, if a franchisee fails, then that franchisee did not follow the franchise system. The franchisee does what it is needed to succeed.

Only you can guide your own personal tolerance for risk and fear. I will say this – a franchise company looks for decisive franchisees who can accept a certain level of risk. This is why the process is a give and take of information – **they are looking at you as much as you are looking at them.** This also is why your risk level is typically reduced by going with a proven franchise system. It is not a guarantee of success, but using a system you have verified to succeed should improve your likelihood of meeting your own goals.

USE THIS VALUABLE FREE WORKSHEET
TO FIND YOUR WINNING FRANCHISE
Download This Free Worksheet Now!
www.TheFranchiseGame.com/bonus

What Is the Best Type of Business for You?

"If you're not a risk taker, you should get the hell out of business."
Ray Kroc, Founder of McDonalds.

For having your own business, numerous options exist. We all have different perceptions of what owning our own business truly means and how that will look. For starting or buying a business, I consider three categories: Independent, Franchise, and Network/Affiliate Marketing. The following is a look at those categories, the advantages and disadvantages of each, and fictional examples of successful and unsuccessful endeavors within each one.

Independent Business

An independent business is just that – the owner started it on his own from the ground up. He likely obtained some type of training, hired expertise, or outsourced necessary expertise to get it started.

Advantages

This option provides complete control to the business owner and allows that person to make all decisions related to the business. This includes changing product lines, advertising mechanisms, etc. The owner answers to no one else. This is ideal for the true entrepreneur.

Disadvantages

The owner must obtain all of the knowledge necessary to be successful in the business. Depending on the type of business, this includes all details for the product line and how to create it, commercial leasing if a location is necessary and all that goes with a build out, marketing and branding expertise, research and development, employee management, and legal details related to the business. It can also be the most expensive path.

Successful Example

Mike was a successful manager with a high end restaurant, and also had a degree in hospitality management. After several years of learning the business, he decided to open his own restaurant. He hired a high-end chef as a partner, hired a commercial realtor to find a location, and hired an attorney to handle the incorporation and contractual issues related to the business. He was not talented in graphic design, so he hired a firm to handle his logos, images, menus, and marketing materials. Ultimately, he grew to five locations and has a catering facility and service as well. It took him a year to get the first business up and running, but he did so successfully.

Unsuccessful Example

Bob is an electrician, and works for an electrical service company. He decides that he is tired of answering to the owner and wants to be on his own. He decides to open Bob's Electrical Services, as he had a few companies that liked his work. He opens the business and the few customers that he kept did give him some business. But one of the customers went out of business – his primary customer. He figures it won't be difficult to get more customers, but he doesn't advertise other than to tell his friends and family about his business, hoping for referrals. After a few months, he closes his doors.

Why did he fail?

Bob did not take the time to truly understand what it takes to be in business. He was more interested in doing the actual work instead of understanding the sales and marketing skills needed to get the work.

Franchise Business

A franchise business is a formal business structure whereby independent business owners purchase the rights to own and run a location of a larger company. The processes and procedures are in place, as well as detailed plans on the location build out, marketing and advertising, hiring plans, etc. Full training is also provided on what the owner needs to know. In return, a royalty is paid to the franchise company for the rights to use the system, as well as the initial franchise fee to get started. (We will discuss the value of these fees in Strategic Move #3).

Advantages

A plan is in place for the franchisee to follow. Systems and processes are duplicated, and expertise is typically at the franchise headquarters to address questions or problems presented by the franchisee. This can range from lease negotiations, the legalities in hiring and firing staff, accounting principles, and advertising choices, just to name a few. Territory protections are typically in place for most companies.

Disadvantages

There are fees involved, yet sometimes these are not considered a disadvantage given the advantages of the expertise and processes in place. The franchisee often is not able to be as creative or have as much flexibility as desired due to the nature of the business. For example, a McDonald's franchisee cannot change the menu. The customers expect to get a Big Mac if they want it. Sometimes a franchisee may find territory restrictions to be limiting.

Successful Example

John is a successful regional sales manager for a software company. He travels more than 50 percent of the work week and is tired of being away from his family. He is also the breadwinner in his family. He cannot afford to leave his job and devote himself full time to his business of choice. He has always wanted to open a small sporting goods store and focus on higher quality equipment. He decided to have a three-year plan to open three locations for a national hair-cutting franchise. The franchise system is meant to be managed more on an absentee basis. He was not passionate about the category, but he could see it as a stepping stone to get what he really wanted. This allowed John to grow an additional income, and leave the job three years later to pursue the sporting goods business. The skills he acquired by being a franchisee transferred to this business and definitely made him more successful.

Unsuccessful Example

Dave was tired of his job and just had to get out. He surfed the net to find a franchise since he had the impression that he would just pay a franchise fee, and the franchise company would do most of the work. Since he likes pizza and heard that it was one of the number one meals ordered in the U.S., he should just open a pizza franchise. The big name companies that he tried to reach would not call him back, but he did get a call from a new pizza franchise that had eight locations in Washington State. Dave lived in Connecticut, so it was a bit challenging for him to get to Washington to see a location. He visited and liked the place well enough, and decided to make the commitment, as he was growing impatient. In the end, he did not review the depth of the new franchise company, and did not realize that they were cash poor and unable to travel to his site to help him. Dave found that he ended up doing most of the work himself. He was working 80-plus hours a week, and not living the life he expected. What Dave really wanted was to spend more time with his family. Now, he rarely sees them. Since he did not consult his wife much about his business decision, you can imagine the tension in the house.

Why did he fail?

Dave made numerous, fairly obvious mistakes. He never took the time to determine what was best for him. In the end, he panicked. He also did not consult with his wife. It is imperative to have your spouse involved early in the process.

Network Marketing or Affiliate Marketing Business

I am adding this category as it is grossly misunderstood. There is such a stigma that a Network Marketing company is a Ponzi scheme. To better understand this business model, please read *The Perfect Business* by Robert Kiyosaki. It is available on CD as well. These companies, the good ones anyway, have quality products. The cost to get started and stay in business is relatively low. In addition, some of the best business and sales training exists in this industry. If you have virtually no funds or assets available to get started in a larger scale business, then start here.

Don't write off this model if you have money as well. You would be amazed how many doctors, dentists, and other professionals use this model for an additional income stream.

I noted Affiliate marketing as it is a close cousin to Network Marketing. Affiliate Marketing takes on numerous forms and is typically an online business option. For example, you can be an affiliate of Amazon and promote their products. You simply are driving traffic to Amazon and want those surfing on the internet to click YOUR link. If they do so and proceed to buy something, then you are paid a commission. This is a huge space and a great way to build a part-time business from home. Investing in the right training is key.

Advantages

Ultra-low cost to get started, and most of what you need with a personal website is available right away so that you can market online. It is truly a matter of how hard you work the business to get the return.

Disadvantages

Low entry can mean low commission and a longer ramp up time to get to the income you desire. Some people are turned off by the industry.

Successful Example

Sara was a successful sales representative for a coffee company when she had her first child. She decided to stay home with her child and proceeded to have two more children. Money was tight, so she decided that they needed more, but she also wanted to be there for her children. She only had about $500 that she could spare for a business. She decided to go with a whole food, repeat business, network marketing company that offered nutritional and health products for adults and children. She liked the message, and worked daily to reach out to people and tell them about the products. She took action with an online marketing program to promote her business, and went to national events as well to stay informed. Sara was able to handle the balance of caring for her children and adding to the household income.

Unsuccessful Example

Mary decided that she wanted to make a little extra money, so she started surfing the Internet for online businesses. She quickly became confused as there was so much out there to implement. She found a plan that allowed her to buy an online marketing kit for $99, and she could get people to buy products from an online mall. What a great deal – no inventory! She bought it, and did some of what she was told in the packet. She thought by just putting up a website that people would find it. When she did not get any sales after a month, she cancelled. She did not realize she was supposed to pay $99 per month to stay active. She never pursued any support from the company, nor did she try to get any education on how to get traffic to her website. She proceeded to tell everyone she knew that online marketing businesses were all scams.

Why did she fail?

Mary made several mistakes. Most importantly, she did not take responsibility for her own decision and lack of effort in the business. I know of solid companies that provide the tools and training necessary to work an online business from home, many requiring no inventory. These can be full time or part time businesses. Like any industry, there are good opportunities and bad opportunities. Get help finding the right one.

Is a Franchise Right for You?

So is a franchise right for you? It is hard to say on the surface. It takes time to actually figure that out. Also, not all franchises are the same. Operating a transmission franchise is highly different than operating a residential cleaning franchise or a sub sandwich franchise. All require completely different financial requirements, employees, real estate, inventory, marketing, and management. The owners are completely different types of people with different goals and skills.

If I could drive home one thing for you to take away from this book, it is this: one of the most important traits to determine about being a franchise owner is whether you can follow a system and follow the rules. It is OK to have new and innovative ideas. Many franchise companies welcome those ideas openly. But in the end, you are buying a system to be followed. I have heard the term "Frantrepreneur," and I am not sure that I truly like it, but it does illustrate the point. A franchisee is not really an entrepreneur. An entrepreneur is the Independent Business Owner who loves the risks associated, but who struggles with following the rules of systems.

With that said, a solid franchisee will need additional skills besides reading the operations manual. The degree of skill will depend on the franchise. For example, the owner of a maid service franchise will need solid sales and customer service skills. The owner will need to develop relationships with customers so that the customer will trust the franchisee and allow the franchisee to send employees to clean the home.

A food franchisee, on the other hand, needs to manage perishable inventory regularly, and must be able to manage numerous employees. The hours for a food establishment are extensive, and coverage is needed on all shifts.

Gets confusing doesn't it? You would be surprised how many people start looking for a food franchise to own just because they know the franchise name. They were not aware that other businesses existed that had a more manageable schedule – one that would require working during the business week with some Saturday mornings, and allow you to be home for dinner each night.

USE THIS VALUABLE FREE WORKSHEET
TO FIND YOUR WINNING FRANCHISE
Download This Free Worksheet Now!
www.TheFranchiseGame.com/bonus

Know How
Franchising Works

*"When you stop chasing the wrong things you give
the right things a chance to catch you."*

~Lolly Daskal

Most newcomers to franchising have several misconceptions regarding what a franchise really is, and how a franchise can benefit a franchisee. The primary things to remember – **a franchise is an established, proven system.** Many will say that it has brand recognition. This can be true for a consumer-based franchise, but that brand recognition is also built through the proven franchise system. New franchises pop up frequently in an area, and with the marketing plan outlined by the franchisor, the brand recognition can build quickly. A business-to-business franchise may never have brand recognition by consumers.

The role of the franchisor is to keep the system growing and running smoothly. Growth comes with new franchisees, and the expanded revenue base of existing franchisees. This growth sometimes comes with the development of new products or services to be implemented by franchisees. All of this takes money – the money that a lot of people think are just "high fees." Let's review three of the primary fees that are often misunderstood.

The Franchise Fee

The initial franchise fee is the price of admission and gives the franchisee the rights to use the system. This fee can vary greatly depending on the type of business. Sometimes it can be on the lower end of about $10,000. Sometimes it is higher – $50,000 to $75,000. The typical franchise fee is closer to $25,000 to $40,000. Don't judge the franchise by the franchise fee! A higher franchise fee may come with a highly sophisticated system and larger territory, as is often the case with business-to-business franchises. The amount charged is typically well justified. It will surprise many to know that the franchisor usually does not make money on the franchise fee. Most of the time, this is a pass-through cost that is used to acquire new franchisees. Finding the right franchisees is not a simple task; it takes numerous resources and time to do all that is necessary to bring a franchisee on board. You want the franchisor to take the time to find the right franchisees – no bad apples to spoil the bunch.

Another benefit of the system that many potential franchisees forget is the access and network instantly created with other franchisees. It can be like a family with most companies, and if everyone is successful, the franchise grows – and each independent franchisee should grow if the system is followed.

The Royalty

The royalty is typically a percentage of the gross revenue that is paid to the franchisor. Sometimes when it makes sense to do so, a franchisor may charge a fixed royalty. There are advantages and disadvantages to each method. This is the oil to keep the engine running. Remember that the franchise company is a business as well, and they are in business to make money. Think of this as expanding the pie for all involved. The franchisee would likely not be in business or as successful in business without the efforts of the franchisor, and the franchisor would not be able to grow without franchisees.

A franchisee must remember that the overhead being supported by the royalty stream of all of the franchisees is a massive benefit. It is more than just paying the bills that the franchisor incurs (yes, they have bills, too). Research and Development is a huge perk for franchisees, and the work is done by the franchisor. Oftentimes a franchisee may have a suggestion for a new product, yet the franchisor puts it into play after developing it. Trying to do this on your own will only deplete your resources. This is often why an independent business can grow stale without innovation, and why franchisees prosper.

The Advertising Fund

The advertising fund fee is probably the most misunderstood fee in franchising. Have you ever noticed all the franchise company ads at sporting events or on television? Have you ever noticed the high quality of those ads, compared to the home grown ads of your local car dealer? The reason they are visible and of such high quality is the advertising fund. Franchisees contribute a percentage of gross sales each month, or the frequency designated by the franchisor. This fund supports the numerous advertising campaigns pursued by the franchisor for the benefit of the franchisees.

The Franchise System –
You Are Expected to Follow It

The franchise is a system to be followed. Franchise candidates must understand that they will not be able to change the system. Committees within the franchise company, comprised of franchisees, often exist for the purpose of suggesting improvements. In the end, it is the franchisor's system for you to follow.

The SALES Process You are Expected to Follow

Franchise companies on the whole follow a basic discovery process. It is essentially a give and take of information so that you as the candidate can obtain the information that you need to make a decision. Your adherence to the process, and how you present yourself to the franchisor, from beginning to end, will determine if you are awarded a franchise if you qualify. This is your first test as a franchisee! Let me repeat that – this is your first test as a franchisee! It is important to follow it and get and A+. This is where many people drop the ball – trust me.

Here are the basic steps that most companies follow:

1. Receive inquiry from candidate

2. Send basic information via the Internet to candidate

3. Reach candidate for introductory interview and prequalification

4. Candidate completes the request for consideration application

5. Franchise Disclosure Document (FDD) is sent to candidate

6. Review of FDD and more detailed information exchanges (lots of time here)

7. Candidate reaches franchisees for validation (lots of time here)

8. Discovery Day/Decision Day

9. Agreements signed

Amazingly, 53 percent of those who inquire about a franchise never make it beyond Step 2! And another 26 percent do not make it beyond Step 4! The reasons are numerous, and usually the person inquiring was just curious, and not serious. However, many candidates make simple mistakes that cause the process to stop as well.

I am not going to review each step in any detail, except to cover concepts that may be new to you. The term FDD is specific to franchising, as well as Discovery Day.

The Franchise Disclosure Document/FDD and Financial Performance Representations

The Franchise Disclosure Document, or "FDD," is the document used for the sale of franchises. The Federal Trade Commission "FTC" requires it, and several states give it more scrutiny before a franchise can be awarded in that state. These are called registration states in the franchise world. This is a non-marketing document. It is a legal document but is supposed to be written in plain English. This is the core of the process, and I actually call it the necessary buzz kill. It is highly important for you to read it and understand it, as it contains what the franchisor is responsible for, what you as a franchisee are responsible for, and most importantly, it contains a copy of the contract that you will sign. There is also an important list – the list of current and past franchisees for you to reach.

There are numerous resources to explain the details of the FDD and how to review it. Here is what I want you to learn for the purposes of this book. The first time you read one, you will be frustrated. The document is written to the advantage of the franchise company. This is where you must continue to evaluate if you are willing to follow a system. The best advice I can give you when reading it – keep in the back of your mind that you want the franchisor to have control over that one rogue franchisee that will make it into the system. It happens and, unfortunately, that is the one who writes on the blogs and tries to ruin the reputation of a good system. As you read the FDD, know that you are one of the solid franchisees in the system, and that you will build a solid business and grow the brand. With that said, I believe you will have a better understanding of what is in the FDD.

There is a section in the FDD titled "Financial Performance Representations." Everyone wants a franchise company to put numbers into the Financial Performance Representations. I am going to give you a background based on my understanding of the Financial Performance Representations and how you should review it, whether it is included or not included.

A Financial Performance Representation typically will give the average revenues across all franchisees. Sometimes, there will be a grouping of the top 25 percent of franchisees, the middle 50 percent, and the lower 25 percent. Many candidates go right to this information, form a conclusion, and decide if they want to review the rest of the document or even the franchise system at all.

I am personally not a fan of Financial Performance Representations. In my humble opinion, I think they can be misused, particularly by franchise brokers. That is a strong statement considering I started out in that part of the industry. I often feel too much weight is put into these numbers.

Why would I say this? Well, why would you want to average all of the franchisees together? There are so many reasons why someone may be in the bottom 25 percent of the revenue averages that you cannot see from just a number. Maybe some of those people only want to make that amount of money! This is so overlooked. What if a franchisee had a goal of making $35,000 out of a business? Let's say for the sake of discussion that this is the lower end of a Financial Performance Representation. Those people did all that they needed to make their goal and they are happy. Doesn't that skew the average? Or you may have others who are busting tail to even make it. Why draw a conclusion just from these numbers alone?

Most of those reviewing a Financial Performance Representations will do just that.

I am more old fashioned, and believe that you need to speak with successful franchisees and pick some randomly on the list. There is such an art to speaking with franchisees – what you should ask and how you should ask it. This is where using a Franchise Coach is extremely helpful.

Discovery Day

Most franchisors have this as a requirement. They want to meet you face to face, as you will likely want to meet them as well, before any final decisions are made. Numerous formats exist, but if the franchise company has it – you need to attend. It is getting close at this point, and if the company decides to award you a franchise, they will want an answer from you typically within five business days after you are informed that a franchise unit has been awarded to you.

A note on "Business Opportunities"

There is a category of investment labeled "business opportunities." These formats are similar to franchises, but much more flexible. They typically allow you to have your own identity and often do not charge a royalty. They are not monitored as closely, nor are they required to give you the entire list of licensees as franchisors must do. It is an area to take caution, but there are some attractive options out there in this space. It can be riskier, but might be a better fit for someone who is more of a true entrepreneur but feels the rigidity of a franchise just does not fit. I know of some solid options in this space as well.

USE THIS VALUABLE FREE WORKSHEET
TO FIND YOUR WINNING FRANCHISE
Download This Free Worksheet Now!

www.TheFranchiseGame.com/bonus

STRATEGIC MOVE #4

Know How Much
You Can Afford

*"Everything you've ever wanted is
on the other side of fear."*

–George Addair

Most businesses that fail do so due to a lack of capital. This is why franchising has an advantage. A franchisor scrutinizes your financial position to make certain that you can afford the franchise. This goes beyond showing that you have just enough to cover the franchise fee.

This is actually where the process can become uncomfortable for the franchise candidate. Your financial statement is personal, and understandably so. However, in order to be awarded a franchise, it must be disclosed. You will thank yourself in the end, as the last thing you want to do is realize at the end of the day that you cannot afford to invest in the business. It will also help you to start fishing in the right pond. If you can only afford to invest $30,000 and you keep researching businesses that require $100,000, then you are looking in the wrong place.

Scrutinize the following asset categories – completely:

Cash – this is all the money you have in checking and savings accounts.

Equity in property – this is typically the equity in your home, but it may be across several properties. In the end, we are trying to find assets that can be leveraged, if needed.

Stocks and Bonds – this includes stocks and bonds that could be liquidated within 30 days. This does not include retirement accounts.

Life Insurance – this includes policies that have cash value; not term life insurance.

Retirement accounts – anything in an IRA, Rollover IRA, Roth IRA, 401k, etc.

I want to spend some time on Retirement Accounts. Programs exist in which, if you qualify, money you have in retirement could be used to INVEST in your business. Notice I said invest. This is not a loan situation. We are taught to not touch our retirement. However, for some people, that is where all of their wealth is held. It is still difficult to get a loan, though lending institutions are lightening up. Scarce lending is particularly true for investments under $250,000. When done properly through the right services, using retirement funds is a fabulous way to go into business with no debt, and to start cash flowing off of that money now. Reach me directly for more details on these programs and the best companies to use. Like any industry, there are good companies and there are bad companies. Just because you see their advertisement doesn't mean they are the best (this goes for franchise companies as well).

When you present your financial statement to a franchisor, you are showing that you are financially qualified to pursue the business. This goes beyond the initial liquid cash requirement. So often candidates will put down just enough to cover the investment – this will disqualify you. The franchisor wants to make certain that you can pay your everyday bills during the ramp up period.

USE THIS VALUABLE FREE WORKSHEET
TO FIND YOUR WINNING FRANCHISE

Download This Free Worksheet Now!

www.TheFranchiseGame.com/bonus

STRATEGIC MOVE #5

How to Get the Franchise Details Needed to Make a Decision

"The most difficult thing is the decision to act,
the rest is merely tenacity."

–Amelia Earhart

The key point is to do what is expected in the process. Don't just window shop, think you will find all that you need to know, and assume you will just be able to contact the franchisor ready to buy. They will still have quite a bit that they want to learn about you.

The best advice is to follow the process, and remember these tips:

- Read the information provided when it is provided.

- Get back with the Franchise Sales person quickly.

- Fill out the Request for Consideration, or whatever the franchisor happens to call it. This is where you must complete your financials. DO THIS ACCURATELY AND COMPLETELY. So many people put in just enough cash that is required for the investment when, in fact, they have more available. Why is this important? The franchisor wants to be certain you can ride out the storm in the beginning. How will you put food on the table if all of your cash is not invested in the franchise fee?

- When you receive the FDD, handle the FDD receipt right away. You want to talk about getting to the front of the line – this is it! It's a battle for just about every Franchise Sales professional I know. Candidates think they are signing the entire agreement. NO! This starts the 14 day clock required by the FTC. It means everything if you want to purchase the franchise. Note that you will not be awarded a franchise without it, and you will likely not receive the password required to speak with franchisees unless it is handled.

These steps are so simple, but 83 percent of candidates violate them. Lastly, if you have decided against the franchise at any time, let the franchisor know. It is just common courtesy.

USE THIS VALUABLE FREE WORKSHEET
TO FIND YOUR WINNING FRANCHISE

Download This Free Worksheet Now!

www.TheFranchiseGame.com/bonus

STRATEGIC MOVE #6

Avoid These Moves and You Will Find a Winner!

"The number one reason people fail in life is because they listen to their friends, family, and neighbors."

~Napoleon Hill

Now that you understand a bit more of the process, let's talk about the mistakes that many candidates make. I often hear from candidates who are truly interested in a franchise, but they are disenchanted with the process. Or, they get to the end of the Discovery Process and they are turned down, and do not understand why.

Now that you have read this far, and should have a better understanding of your ability to be a business owner, we have reached the crux of the reason why I wrote this book.

A little background again. Since 2008, I have progressed to the role of Franchise Sales for a few companies. This role is sometimes called Business Development, Franchise Development, Franchise Sales, etc. In the end, I am taking numerous candidates through the franchise sales process to determine if they are a fit for a specific franchise, and ultimately approve or decline them for the business. It has been a recent trend in franchising to outsource the sales function to people like me. To get the best resources that are truly exceptional at awarding franchises to the right people is an expensive endeavor for a franchise. Outsourcing is a solid solution, so don't be concerned if you talk with someone in a similar role. You are likely in good hands.

I have worked with several companies in this role. My most noteworthy client was recently named the No. 1 New Franchise by Entrepreneur Magazine. The company went from three units in 2007 to more than 300 at the end of 2012, and they are approaching 600 as we enter 2015. The company is called Kona Ice®. A nice company with a spin on an old favorite – the ice cream truck. The primary product sold is shaved ice.

Some of you just made the conclusion that Kona Ice® is a summer-only business. You will be surprised to know that summer typically ranks third out of the four seasons, and when desired, franchisees in the northern states are functional in the winter months. Remember what I said about drawing early conclusions?

What an exciting experience to be part of the progression of this company. Most importantly, I have a huge appreciation for how candidates present themselves in the franchise discovery process. Some of the things that people do is astounding, some of it downright funny, and some of it appalling.

Franchises are Awarded, Not Sold

Here is the primary problem for most candidates. They do not understand that franchises are AWARDED, not SOLD. This is so important for candidates to understand that I will repeat it – franchises are AWARDED, not SOLD. You have the final say as to whether you will BUY it, but you cannot BUY it unless it is OFFERED to you first.

Sound like a similar process? (Hint – cannot accept a job unless it is offered to you).

Why is this so important? Franchisors are looking for people to be business partners with them, and to be the face and image of the company with the public. Franchisors are looking for candidates with the right blend of skills for their specific business, and as we stated, this can vary across companies.

Since candidates go into the process thinking they are simply a buyer, they tend to approach it with the incorrect temperament. In the franchise sales process, you will not be dealing with a car salesman trying to sell a car to everyone walking in the door, so don't treat the process as such. You do not buy a franchise in a day. It typically takes at least 30 days and up to 90 days to go through the entire discovery process and reach a decision on both ends. It can be as little as 30 days if you use a Franchise Coach and make it priority one to make a decision.

So remember that as you pursue a franchise, keep in mind that any franchise worth its salt will be evaluating you as much as you will be evaluating them. It truly is about mutual consideration. Here are some basic qualities they are seeking:

A. Team player and professional presentation

B. Ability to follow a process and a system (sound familiar)

C. Financially qualified to pursue the business

Franchisors receive hundreds of requests per week. They do not have time to waste on the curious, less than serious, and particularly those not qualified. Window shoppers are easily dropped, as they typically disqualify themselves anyway.

In the end, even though you are not looking for a "job", you need to treat the process as you would if you were going to the job "awarding" process.

Top Ways to Blow It with a Franchise

I have a somewhat humorous list that I send to candidates to illustrate what many people do when they ask for information on a franchise and how they respond when I reach them. There are numerous ways to blow it, but remember that franchisors receive hundreds of requests per week. When I handle a candidate request, that person starts out as a "10" but below is how he or she can instantly be knocked down to a "5" or less.

The candidate called franchisees right away – before ever speaking with me.

> **Why this is a problem:** This is so frustrating. Good intentions by those wanting to review the business as they just want to get to the bottom line. However, you likely found that the franchisee would not talk to you. Most have passwords now, and headquarters wants to make certain that candidates are prescreened before speaking with franchisees. It is <u>not</u> the role of the franchisee to work with you at the beginning of your review in the business. And – if you made the Queen Mother of mistakes and called the local franchisee, one of two things probably happened: he told you that he already owns the entire area (likely not true), or he proceeded to call headquarters and secure the area that you wanted.

> **Better actions:** Be patient – get educated on the business and see if you qualify first. It does not take long to get to the point of reaching franchisees, and you will handle the call better if you wait.

Answer the phone and say "Sorry, I cannot talk – I am in a meeting right now."

Why this is a problem: You just told the franchise developer that you are not very serious about this specific franchise or possibly a business at all. If you are in a meeting that is so important, why did you answer the phone? This is a bigger issue than you might think. Would you exhibit the same behavior if the head of Human Resources just called you for an interview for your dream job? Probably not – you would leap out of that meeting as quickly as possible. In the end, you just told the franchise developer that you are a tire kicker and not really serious about the business. Hence, they just moved to the next person who inquired, and will wait to hear from you.

Better actions: This goes to general courteous behavior. We are so accessible now due to our cell phones. It is OK to let a call go to voice mail – that is why you have voice mail! If a meeting is so important, treat it as such. Or, if you realize that it is a franchise company getting BACK with you after YOU submitted a request, just as if it were the HR representative for a job, treat it professionally. Something like this is better: "I am so pleased that you have reached me. I wanted to take your call quickly to let you know that I am not able to talk right at this moment, but I am eager to speak with you." Isn't that a better impression?

Tell the franchisor that you just wanted information and you will decide later

Why this is a problem: You appear to be the eternal tire kicker, and you review a franchise like you would a book – by the cover. As you hopefully realize by now, a franchise purchase is not decided in a vacuum. The franchisor is looking at you as much as you are looking at them. Were you one of those people who thought a Kona Ice® territory was only valuable in the south?

Better actions: Allow the salient points to be discussed, and follow the discovery process to truly make an informed decision.

Don't show up for a scheduled phone appointment or, even worse, never respond to the initial email contact or phone call.

Why this is a problem: By not showing up for an appointment, you are not showing good judgment and professionalism. We all know that things happen and schedules can change. Treat the franchisor as you would like to be treated – let them know if you cannot make it.

Better actions: Keep your appointments. Make it right as soon as possible. If you have decided against the franchise at this point, say so. Don't give the lame "we decided to go in a different direction." Tell them why you really decided against it. You may have made a truly invalid assumption, and you should give the franchisor a chance to make certain that you are making an informed decision with accurate information. It makes my toes curl to think of how many people missed out on a great business by making their own uninformed assumptions.

Unprofessional voice mail message (e.g., jokes, vulgar music, etc). Or worse – you give your home number, but others in the home are rude to the franchisor when they call.

Why this is a problem: Simply unprofessional. Remember, the franchisor is getting back with hundreds of people a week. What kind of an image is portrayed with vulgar music? And you are hoping to be a business owner? Or if you have a corny home message where you are trying to trick the caller into thinking he or she is really talking to you. The franchisor moves to the next person – and rapidly. I have disqualified candidates simply because of the message they have on their voice mail.

Better actions: Use a professional voice mail message. It is often the first impression that you make. If you must use your home number, alert those answering the phone so that they answer professionally as well. Better yet, just provide your personal cell phone. Be careful to answer it only when you are ready to really take the call, as noted above.

Complain about the franchise fees and royalties without having a solid understanding of why and how franchising works.

Why this is a problem: If you spend your time with an attitude about the fees, you have illustrated that you are against the idea from the start. Yes, you must make certain that the fees are in line with what you are receiving. But tread lightly here as many blow it without realizing it.

Better actions: Get educated on what a franchise is all about and be careful where you get your advice. A franchise expands the pie for all involved, and the fees are actually a bargain!

You take the position that you expect the franchisor to do all of the work – after all, it is your money.

Why this is a problem: You must be educated about being in business in general. So many people think that the franchise company does all of the work for "all of those fees." This goes back to the erroneous perception that the franchisor is beholden to you for making an investment, instead of realizing the pie is expanding for all involved with a solid franchise.

Better actions: Understand what it takes to be in business and, during your discovery process, determine if you are receiving the value expected for your investment. Also realize that you will have to do work in the business as well.

Multi-tasking while on the phone – shuffling papers, doing dishes, etc. And the ultimate no-no: flushing the toilet while talking on the phone.

Why this is a problem: Do I really need to explain this one? This goes to the point about being so accessible with the age of cell phones, plus being professional. If you cannot talk or have distractions, or need to step away for a moment, say so. At least once a week, someone flushes the toilet during our conversation.

Better actions: Be focused on the conversation.

When the franchisor calls and you say "I am at work right now – you will have to call in the evening."

Why this is a problem: You just told the franchise company you do not have time to run a business. The franchise company does not have representatives working around the clock 24 hours a day, 7 days a week. Remember, you are trying to stand out, not get bumped to the bottom of the list. This can be challenging, and you are trying to sort through numerous opportunities yourself. This is where the later section on getting help finding the right franchise will be helpful to you.

Better actions: Find the time to speak with the company. You would find the time if you were looking for a job.

Refusal to complete the financial statement – including your "investors" and "family that will help."

Why this is a problem: This is a big one. I can appreciate that you want to keep your financial position private. It just does not work in the franchise discovery process. The franchisor needs to know early on that you can financially proceed with the business should you be awarded one, and you choose to accept. You do not want to waste your time on concepts that are out of reach financially. It just is not productive.

Another big one – I have "partners willing to invest when I find the right thing," or "my family is willing to help." I can tell you this rarely works out and is a big red flag. Those wanting to invest have to then go through every part of the discovery process. A solid franchisor will insist these people are involved – from step 1.

Better actions: Fill out the financial application ACCURATELY. It is important that the franchisor can see your entire financial picture. If a franchise company requires that you have $30,000 in cash to invest, they should not allow you to continue if you only have $30,000 to your name. It would just be irresponsible. You need extra money in the bank to live! One reason franchise companies succeed is because they verify that franchisees are well qualified financially. A franchise company can often get creative on financing with equity in property or your retirement accounts (without penalty and withholding costs). In the end – fill it out. If you use a franchise coach, that person will expect the same and can be of tremendous assistance.

Do not follow the process outlined by the franchisor to review the business.

Why this is a problem: By not following the process outlined, you give the impression you will not follow the franchise system as well. **This is your first test on being a solid franchisee.** It is important to get an A+.

Better actions: Follow the process with a smile on your face and address all conversations, both verbal and non-verbal, with complete enthusiasm and mutual respect. If you don't receive it in return from the franchisor, then move on. Remember – you cannot purchase a franchise unless it is awarded to you first, just like you cannot accept a job offer that is not offered to you.

Asking your advisors the wrong questions. Don't ask your attorney or accountant if you should buy the franchise.

Why this is a problem: This will be a bold statement. Most of what you need to know to buy the franchise will be compiled through information obtained directly from the franchisor, and by those in their system – the franchisees. I am not saying that you should not seek advice from others – just be cautious. Those you are speaking to – do they know business and, especially, do they understand franchising?

Better actions: I could write an entire book just on this section, but I will keep it brief. For attorneys, make certain you consult a franchise attorney. The laws are specific and unique, and if you use a general attorney, they will just cost you time and aggravation, and you could miss out on a great business. For accountants, consult with one familiar with the benefits of the franchise fee and the royalties. An accountant's role is to tell you if you can be profitable, and when. Regarding both the attorney and accountant – do not ask them if you should buy the business! They are always more inclined to say no – it is safer.

The big message is to remember their own personal interests for advising you. Same for friends and family. Are they still in dream mode themselves? Are they more envious that you are taking steps to change your life? Just take caution here. I have seen many candidates miss out on great opportunities when they received misguided advice from their so called advisors.

You may be surprised by the simplicity of this list, but I cannot stress strongly enough the importance of it. By watching out for these simple behaviors, you will be amazed how far you will get in the process, and how quickly.

USE THIS VALUABLE FREE WORKSHEET
TO FIND YOUR WINNING FRANCHISE
Download This Free Worksheet Now!
www.TheFranchiseGame.com/bonus

Don't Go It Alone:
How to be Awarded
the Best Franchise for You

*"Two roads diverged in a wood, and I—I took the one less traveled by,
And that has made all the difference."*

–Robert Frost

Do some of the soul searching steps mentioned in this book. I would imagine that you are surprised by the list of ways people blow it. The list can be longer, but I focused on what candidates do **early** in the process and why they do not get the information they need to decide. You also need to take a hard look at the time and money you have available, and if you have been fishing in the wrong pond all along.

Don't take weeks and months to do it. You don't want to be in a perpetual state of learning to learn. You want to take action and get to the point of making a decision and actually starting that business. Stop window shopping!

So how can you make a purchasing decision with so many options available to you? It is paramount that you tap into the expertise of a Franchise Coach. Look at all of the steps necessary just to complete the due diligence for one company, along with the 14 day clock for the FDD review. The key is understanding what is truly important, how much you can afford, and what is the SHORT list of companies that will meet that criteria. In addition, is the territory in your area available? Or even better, if your current area is sold, maybe it is for sale, but not publicly. Franchisors sell a location for a franchisee all the time, but they do not go through a business broker. The company gets enough leads, including those from the Franchise Coaching community. Don't just look at the list of locations and think that you do not have options.

Using a Franchise Coach is a wise step. You may find that to be self-serving. Now that I have seen all sides – being a Franchise Coach, a Franchise Sales Developer, and a franchisee, I know the value in the coaching sessions to get candidates to the right SHORT list of companies. It is a lengthy process, particularly if you do it on your own. Most candidates simply do not understand what the companies are looking for in a candidate, and the candidate fails to present himself or herself accordingly. A Franchise Coach will make sure you start with the right list based on what you think you want at the moment, and coach you on how to follow the entire discovery process.

It does not cost you any additional funds to use a Franchise Coach. They are compensated by the franchise company. The benefits of the guidance and the direct introductions to the companies are well worth it for you to capitalize on the free service.

Franchise companies enjoy using Franchise Coaches as it helps their Franchise Developers to focus on qualified candidates. Everyone wins – particularly you. Finding a Franchise Coach you trust can be a challenge. It is a transient industry, and you will easily find Franchise Brokers who have been in the business for less than six months and leave the industry in less than a year. To be an effective coach, he or she must spend a tremendous amount of time learning about the franchise companies and what they offer.

It is definitely not necessary to use someone local to you. It is far better to find one who is actually trying to listen to you and guide you to the right business. A good amount of your interactions, even with the franchisors, will be over the phone. Your research will be done on the Internet. A good coach will tell you if they cannot help you. A good coach will also help you with your search in general, even if you are pursuing companies not actively engaged with the Franchise Broker or Franchise Coaching community.

My company is still actively involved, and thriving in this environment of finding the right business for people just like you, including franchises, business opportunities, network marketing, and online businesses. Contact me at Colleen@TheFranchiseGame.com and I will be happy to have a preliminary discussion with you.

The worst that will happen – you will find a way to make money you were not aware of before reaching us.

Decide to be serious this time around, and find a winner!

FIND YOUR WINNER
USE THIS VALUABLE FREE WORKSHEET TO SHIFT
THROUGH THE DUDS AND FIND YOUR WINNER
Download This Free Worksheet Now!

www.TheFranchiseGame.com/bonus

Recommended Reading

The E-Myth by Michael E. Gerber

Lead...For God's Sake by Todd Gongwer

Rich Dad, Poor Dad by Robert Kyosaki

The Perfect Business by Robert Kyosaki

The Slight Edge by Jeff Olson